design ideas for your home

inspired by the National Trust

design ideas for your home

inspired by the National Trust

Alison Dalby

National Trust

First published in the United Kingdom in 2013 by
National Trust Books
10 Southcombe Street
London W14 0RA

An imprint of Anova Books Company Ltd

ISBN 9781907892493

A CIP catalogue record for this book is available from the British Library.

21 20 19 18 17 16 15 14 13
10 9 8 7 6 5 4 3 2 1

Reproduction by Mission Productions Ltd, Hong Kong
Printed and bound by 1010 Printing International Ltd, China

This book can be ordered direct from the publisher at the website www.anovabooks.com, or
try your local bookshop. Also available at National Trust shops and shop.nationaltrust.org.uk.

Page 2: The elegant colour scheme in the hall
at Peckover House contributes to a welcoming
first impression.

Right: A detail of the upper hallway ceiling at
Red House.

contents

introduction

Anyone who loves homes and interiors will find a wealth of ideas in the National Trust's historic houses, as well as a fascinating insight into the decorative tastes of the past. This book brings together some of the National Trust's most inspiring room schemes, colour palettes and displays, which can be copied, adapted or simply used as a starting point for an exciting new look in your own home.

If you have a penchant for contemporary interiors, don't let the word 'historic' put you off. From elegant townhouses and cosy cottages to open-plan Modernist gems and some of the Trust's most beautiful holiday homes, you'll find plenty of design inspiration here for any interior. Unless you are faithfully restoring a period property, or live in a listed building, which may restrict what you can do, there's almost no limit to the extraordinary designs you can draw on for guidance and ideas. The tips in this book will help you decide which colours and styles might work for you, while the source list at the back provides the details of some of the companies and products that will help you 'get the look'.

Whether you're guided just by the images or choose to visit a property that has appealed to you, I hope you'll enjoy viewing these interiors in a new light and seeing how some of the styles and schemes might work in your own home.

Alison Dalby

Left: An inviting decorative scheme was designed for the dining room at Portland House holiday cottage.

finding inspiration

You may already have a clear idea of your style preferences and the look you want to achieve in your home, since most of us have our favourite colours or are drawn to particular patterns and designs. However, if you're unsure about how to develop an idea for a room, putting together a mood board will help you to identify your personal style so that you can plan a scheme that's right for you.

Start by gathering pictures or clippings of things that appeal to you. Inspiration can come from anywhere: postcards of interiors and architecture, photographs of sunsets and flowers, cuttings from fashion magazines or catalogues, attractive packaging or actual samples of fabric, paint and wallpaper.

Once you have all your pictures and swatches you can start to build your ideas and give them some focus. Stick your favourite examples on to a large piece of paper or card, or a pin-board on the wall, and see what themes they prompt – you might be surprised by what stands out.

Knowing the styles and colour schemes that you feel comfortable with will enable you to choose products with confidence. It may even inspire you to try something different, even daring, and create a whole new look for your home.

Right: A mood board will help you to identify your personal style.

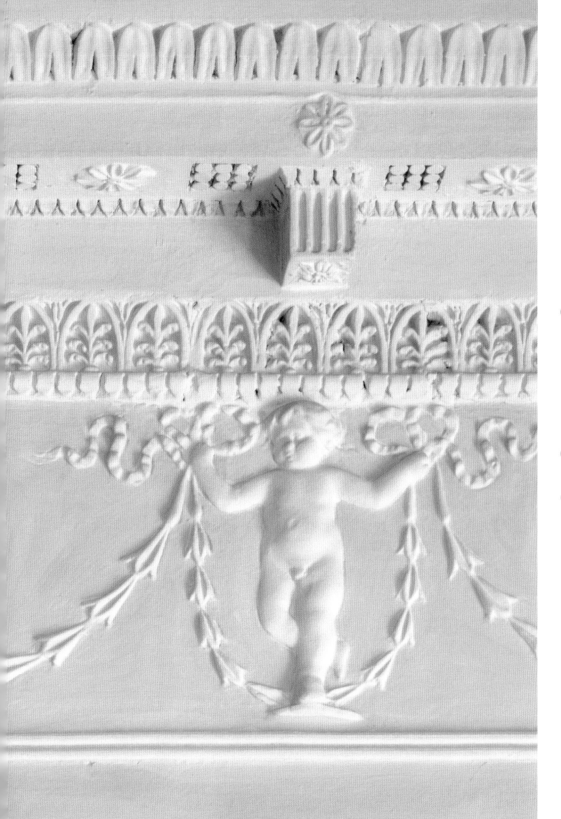

inspired by the past

townhouse elegance

The image of the 18th-century Georgian townhouse that springs to mind is one of elegance and gracious living, with large sash windows and shutters, painted panelling, muted colour schemes and a wealth of plaster swags and urns.

Architecture inspired by classical Greece and Rome gave the defining look to the era, but the period witnessed a number of interior styles and fashions. The feminine and playful Rococo was skilfully worked into asymmetrical and curvaceous carving for mirrors, picture frames and fancy plasterwork.

The exotic styles of the East were also popular in ranges of furniture and decorative accessories from Chinese wallpapers (see page 117) to ceramics and lacquered cabinetry. In some homes this was the chosen scheme, in glamorous bedrooms and dressing-rooms for example.

Yet despite the crossover in styles, the classical look prevailed, and many 18th-century home owners wanted this style, turning to the light touch and delicate adaptation of its features inspired by architect Robert Adam. The motifs on his stucco work and decoration for chimneypieces, ceilings and panels included garlands, vases, flowers, ribbons, griffins and nymphs.

Peckover House in Cambridgeshire is among the finest surviving 18th-century townhouses. Its characteristic features are evident in the entrance hall with its meticulous proportions and tranquil colour scheme of verditer green and white, but it also shows examples of the most capricious Rococo style in the elaborately carved mirror-frame in the drawing room.

A feast of inspiration lies behind the terracotta exterior of poet William Wordsworth's childhood home in Cumbria. There's an appealing colour palette in every room, with soft green in the dining-room and primrose yellow in one of the bedrooms, and comfortable antique furniture adds the finishing touches. The interiors are also decorated with pretty wallpaper and dainty sprig fabrics that embody the look of the time.

One of the crown jewels of townhouse sophistication, its interiors filled with inspiring ideas, is Mompesson House in the Cathedral Close in Salisbury. With panelled rooms, richly embellished by elaborate plasterwork, and cosy parlours and bedrooms in their 18th-century colours, this is an irresistible combination of refinement and homely charm.

Above: The elegant dining room at Mompesson House.

Left: The window recess in the drawing room at Peckover House.

Far left: One of the pretty bedrooms at Wordsworth House.

arts and crafts style

Few names in design have had as enduring an appeal as that of William Morris, the pioneer of the Arts and Crafts Movement. Many of his fabrics and wallpapers are still available – some ranges are in traditional Arts and Crafts colours and patterns, others are in new shades with a modern twist and many more are simply inspired by the look.

The Arts and Crafts Movement was born out of a desire to return to quality craftsmanship that was prompted by the mass-production of objects in an increasingly industrialised Victorian Britain. Morris's circle of friends included architect Philip Webb and Dante Gabriel Rossetti, founder member of the Pre-Raphaelites, a group of artists who shared a passion for medieval romance and imagery. At Red House, Morris's home in Bexleyheath, surviving examples of the painted decoration that he and his friends applied to walls and items of furniture show a huge outpouring of creativity and a love of the medieval past that inspired the Arts and Crafts style.

Morris also drew heavily on birds, animals and flowers for his inspiration. The garden at Red House inspired an early pattern he called 'Trellis', and soon a plethora of fabrics, wallpapers, furniture and other products were available through the firm Morris & Co. Standen in Sussex and Wightwick Manor in Wolverhampton are among the homes in which the Arts and Crafts influence can be found in abundance.

Standen has rooms decorated in Morris wallpapers and fabrics alongside hand-embroidered wallhangings by some of the female members of the family who lived there. Their work is complemented by painted panelling, a key feature of the style, along with other furnishings, tiles and lamps now synonymous with the era. The rooms show how the textures, colours and patterns of the Arts and Crafts style worked together so harmoniously.

At Wightwick Manor, thirteen rooms are decorated in distinctive patterns from Morris's company, some displaying romantic Pre-Raphaelite paintings. Lines of poetry by Tennyson and Walter Scott were painted on to plain fire-surrounds and around the ceilings, adding extra charm and a personal touch.

'Arts and Crafts' has become a byword for skilled craftsmanship and organic fabric designs. At its heart lay a desire to return to nature and the handiwork of the artisan that has a strong resonance again today.

Left: The sitting room at Coleton Fishacre.

Right: The glamorous Art Deco bathroom at Upton House.

modernist marvels

While the Modernist Movement is almost a century old, it perhaps has more of a resonance today than ever before. Its clean, simple, streamlined rooms provide an appealing counterbalance to a hectic pace of life.

Modernism flowered after the First World War, rejecting historical precedent and excessive ornamentation in favour of new technology and materials. Many talented designers emerged from Continental Europe, keen to be part of this new style. Among them was Hungarian émigré Ernö Goldfinger, who built a terrace of three houses in Willow Road in London's Hampstead in the 1930s and occupied the middle home with his family. Around the same time, young architect Patrick Gwynne persuaded his parents to let him demolish their

Victorian house and build a Modernist replacement instead – The Homewood, in Surrey. Both houses embody all the energy and innovation of the style.

Modernist ideas included the creation of adaptable and split-level spaces which could be enlarged or divided by folding screens and moveable partitions. Simplicity was encouraged by built-in, foldaway and fitted furniture and storage, removing any inclination for clutter. Most Modernist architects also designed furniture, including ground-breaking designs in tubular steel, bent plywood timber and leather, many of which are now much copied and mass-produced for today's interiors.

The optimum use of natural light was also a Modernist feature and full-height windows are as much an element of the interior design as the furniture. The effect of merging indoors and out was enhanced by avoiding fussy window treatments and the choice of simple drapes or blinds.

Left: The living room at The Homewood.

Right: A split-level, light-filled interior at 2 Willow Road.

Below: Tulip light fittings designed for The Homewood.

journey through time

For a journey through the past, Avebury Manor in Wiltshire offers something a little different to most historic houses. Nine richly atmospheric rooms are the result of an innovative approach to design, having become the focus for the 2011 BBC TV series *The Manor Reborn*.

The series followed a team of historians, designers, specialist craftspeople and volunteers as they decorated and refurbished the empty 500 year-old Manor and brought it back to life, reflecting various periods in its history from Tudor to the eve of the Second World War.

Each room captures the essential look of its era, telling the fascinating tales of the Manor's former inhabitants. A cosy Tudor parlour fitted with tapestries and lush woven matting contrasts with a luxurious Georgian dining room with hand-painted Chinese wallpaper and a stylish Jazz Age sitting room with Art Deco furniture.

Some of the rooms illustrate decorative paint effects of the past, which are still practised today. Marbling on wall panels and a delicate ceiling design of blue sky and clouds in the sumptuous Queen Anne bedchamber are just some of the extraordinary results achieved by modern specialist painters that have added to the glamour and flair of this unique house.

Top: The Queen Anne bedchamber with its rich colour scheme.

Above: The cosy Tudor parlour.

Left: The Governor of Jamaica's dining room.

colour

colour

Colour has always been at the heart of interior design. As a result, historic houses of different periods and styles offer a fabulous source of ideas for colour schemes today.

- Daylight and artificial light affect the appearance of colour. When choosing paint, buy tester pots, apply paint to a large sheet of paper and stick it on the wall. Observe the effect at different times of the day.
- Consider which direction your windows face when making your colour choice. In the northern hemisphere, a north-facing room without much sun will benefit from light tones from the warm side of the colour wheel, such as yellow or peach. A brighter, south-facing room in the northern hemisphere will suit shades from both sides of the colour wheel, but for a cool, airy feel, try pale hues of blue or green.
- There are no hard-and-fast rules but, generally speaking, dark colours tend to advance, making them a good choice if you want a room to feel cosier or smaller. Lighter colours usually recede, creating an impression of space.
- Sometimes the best plan is to work with the limitations of a room. A small or naturally dark room can look sumptuous in rich, warm colours that emphasise its cosiness.

The most important thing is to have fun with colours. Choose those that you feel comfortable with and that help you achieve the right mood and atmosphere for each room in your home.

Top: Robert Adam's 1760 design for the painted breakfast room in the family pavilion at Kedleston Hall.

Above: *Jane (Jeanie) Elizabeth Hughes, Mrs Nassau Senior*, by George Frederick Watts, at Wightwick Manor.

Right: Lady Iliffe's bedroom at Basildon Park.

choosing colours

If you are unsure which colours might work in your home there are three basic types of scheme you can consider. A colour wheel, like the one shown right, is a useful guide to picking your favourite combinations.

Monochrome: A monochrome scheme is created from different shades of one colour (such as dark blue and pale blue). A scheme of this type can be the easiest to put together but texture is important (see page 124). These schemes can include one-colour patterned fabrics and wallpapers.

Analogous: The colours that sit next to each other on the wheel (such as green and blue) produce a harmonious look, tending to work best when one colour is dominant and the others are used in smaller amounts.

Complementary: These colours sit opposite each other on the wheel (such as green and red or blue and orange) and can produce exciting schemes with plenty of contrast. Try one as the dominant colour, with the other in a more muted shade or in smaller quantities so that the effect is not overpowering, or choose softer shades of each.

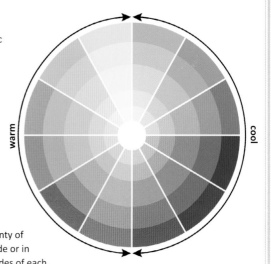

warm

cool

blue

From navy and cornflower to turquoise and duck egg, the effects of blue can be rich and alluring or soft and serene.

- For centuries, shades of blue were extracted from woad plants and those of the indigo genus.
- The semi-precious stone lapis lazuli was highly prized for its vivid blue colour and was ground to a powder to make paint.
- The fashion in Europe for blue-and-white Chinese ceramics began in the 17th century.
- One of the first synthetic pigments was Prussian blue, manufactured in the early 18th century.
- In Neo-classical interiors, clear blue was a popular colour against plasterwork picked out in white.
- The whitewash used on the walls of many Victorian kitchens was tinted blue as the colour was believed to repel flies.
- William Morris revived the interest in natural dyes such as those used for blue by employing them in his fabric designs.

Above left: This stunning blue interior is from an early 1800s travelling chariot, part of a collection at Arlington Court's Carriage Museum.

Above: An elegant blue decorative scheme in the drawing room at Ormesby Hall.

Left: The blue-and-white kitchen tiles at Treasurer's House.

blue schemes

Blue will work in many settings and, depending on the shade, it can be classically stylish or crisp and invigorating.

The charming blue-patterned Arts and Crafts wallpaper at Wallington creates the backdrop to an elegant parlour (above). White woodwork and panelling keep the scheme fresh and lively, making a sophisticated contrast to the dark wood furniture and gilt-framed pictures.

A seaside feel has been achieved in this Cornish holiday cottage at Mowhay (above) by teaming bold blue walls with cheerful sunny curtains, while bare floorboards and pine furniture give a rustic touch. Painted white, the beamed ceiling prevents the vibrant walls from becoming too overpowering.

At 2 Willow Road (above), Modernist architect Ernö Goldfinger used bold blue alongside white in the guest bedroom. The blue wall behind the foldaway bed is on show only when the bed is in use; when the white doors conceal it and those around the basin are shut, the room returns to a more neutral scheme once again, the red chair giving the décor a dash of energy.

A stylish pairing of blue and terracotta has given this dining room at Park Cottage holiday house a rather modern twist (above). The white picture rail has formed a natural division between the two colours, a clever trick to offer the impression of a lower ceiling. The red seat covers on the chairs and the tiles around the fireplace provide extra warm touches.

blue and white

Above: Bed hangings in sky-blue silk bring gentle colour to this pearl-coloured bedroom at Mompesson House. The red-patterned carpet has grounded the scheme and, with the dark wood furniture, has emphasised the room's Georgian style and elegance. This scheme would work equally well with bed hangings in a polka-dot or floral blue-and-white design, or another pastel colour such as pink.

Left: Blue-and-white Delftware has become a design classic that adds charm to many interior styles. At Packwood House, clever use is made of two tile designs, with detailed patterns halfway up the wall to define the bath area and then smaller, simpler images above. Patterned accessories, such as the towels, have brought more blue and white into the scheme.

Above: A blue-and-white combination gets extra impact with gold detailing around white-painted windows that have been left undressed. The patterned rug, with its strong blue elements, ties this Berrington Hall scheme neatly together.

Above: The blue-and-white combination in this bedroom at Godolphin holiday cottage doesn't dominate the room but is part of a harmony of colours and textures. The coffee-coloured bed drapes, patterned curtains and rugs have added extra colour to the mix, but the blues are picked up at different points, with blue and white echoed in the bedspread and in the lamp and plates on display.

Above: Stencilling has a long history but enjoyed a revival with other paint effects in the 1980s. At the Back to Backs in Birmingham a delicate blue and black floral wall design has also been used as a dado-rail effect. If you don't wish to embark on stencilling, wallpaper in a similar design would provide an equally attractive look.

a touch of blue

If you want to experiment with strong shades of blue, begin with small accents of the colour in your room.

A white kitchen at Portland House holiday cottage (above) gets an injection of colour with bright blue worktops and roller blinds. Replacing worktops and adding new accessories are cost-effective ways to refresh a kitchen and allow you to bring vibrant new colours into your scheme.

Blue is the striking colour in the dining room at Nuffield Place (left), but it's also the most transient: in the form of delicate

glassware for the table it shows how a splash of bold colour can transform a room in an instant and create memorable impact for a special occasion.

A little blue goes a long way in a few well-chosen objects for display around a white fireplace at Standen (above). Here, patterned blue tiles have been framed to provide an interesting piece of art on the wall above.

the 'wow' factor

An intense Prussian blue creates eye-popping impact at Lindisfarne Castle, re-designed in the early 20th century by Sir Edwin Lutyens. Contrasted against arching stone walls and a terracotta herringbone-tiled floor, it gives a rich and theatrical effect, offset by the shining brass chandelier (reflected in the mirror) and gleaming wall-lanterns.

This is a daring use of intense colour, so if you're unsure about it for a whole room, try experimenting with a feature wall. Alternatively, dip a toe in the water and opt for a few bold blue cushions or throws in a neutral scheme.

green

Olive, teal, apple and lime are some of the shades in the green palette and can create soothing or energising schemes.

- Lincoln green was the name of a bright green dyed woollen cloth, associated with Robin Hood and his men.
- The ancient Egyptians used the mineral malachite for green paints – and even for their eye make-up.
- Throughout the 18th century the Georgians used different shades of green, including olive and pea green.
- Arts and Crafts designers loved using green – they drew heavily on nature and the outdoors for their inspiration.
- Emerald green, a pigment based on arsenic, was used from 1814 for paint, fabrics and wallpapers until its toxic effects were acknowledged.
- Eau de nil ('water of the Nile'), a pale yellowish green, was an elegant choice for many 1930s interiors.

Left: A cosy corner at Cherryburn shows how moss green and olive are ideal for muted colour schemes.

Above: A serene green colour scheme is shown in the painting *The Library at Chancellor's House*, by Florence Seth, displayed at Belton House.

Shades of green

A miniature of Elizabeth I (left) against a background of green damask in the green closet at Ham House. Experiment with a strong shade like this for cushions or throws to add a 'pop' of colour.

Grey-green is soft and restful, and very effective when mixed with floral chintz and crisp white linen.

Lime, apple and mint greens work well with bright blue or gleaming white for a fresh, contemporary feel, as seen in the morning lounge at Portland House holiday cottage (left).

Sage green creates a warm atmosphere, especially when teamed with splashes of burnt orange and gilt-framed mirrors and pictures.

green schemes

Associated with the colours of nature, green shades can bring a tranquil outdoor atmosphere to a room.

Moss-green velvet curtains and layers of texture from throws, rugs and cushions have created a relaxed and bohemian feel at Bradley (above). Green notes from the framed picture and the potted plants and flowers add to the effect.

Muted green panelling is complemented here by the pinky-red, patterned chintz sofa and the matching green cushions (above). Velvet curtains in burnt orange have added a strong contrast, picking out highlights of similar colours in the patterned rug at Sudbury Hall.

White is often chosen for the decorative schemes in beamed cottages, but other colours can offer exciting design alternatives. For her sitting-room walls at Monk's House, writer Virginia Woolf chose a striking apple green that is crisp and uplifting (above). The colour is echoed in the patterned upholstery and accessories.

green and white

One of the most successful colour combinations is green and white, which suits almost any style of interior.

This bedroom at Housesteads holiday cottage (above) is a lively mix of grassy green florals, spotted and plain fabrics and accessories which bring splashes of country colour to a neutral backdrop.

An elegant Georgian feel is achieved at Godolphin holiday cottage (above), where rich green panelling and cornices and floral-sprigged curtains blend with a simple black iron bedstead and cream bedcover.

Green and white makes a great colour choice for bathrooms. At Lyme Park (above), bands of dark and light green tiles decorate the wall and add just the right amount of colour and interest. Positioned three-quarters of the way up the wall, they also appear to lower the high ceiling.

If your room isn't overlooked, windows don't always need curtains or blinds. With the recess painted white, and with fresh green walls, the decorative scheme at A La Ronde echoes the colours of the garden and creates the effect of fusing indoors and out (above).

focus on green

Standen, a homely and welcoming Arts and Crafts house, was designed by architect Philip Webb for the Beale family in the last years of the 19th century. While many of the rooms show the impact that can be achieved with wallpapers, the dining room is a simpler scheme based on dark green painted panelling, which makes the ideal backdrop to a collection of blue-and-white porcelain and richly textured curtains and rugs.

When the curtains are closed in the evening, with the glow from lamps and candles, the room takes on a warm, cosy atmosphere for dinner and entertaining. However, the fresh white above the picture-rail and across the ceiling gives the room a lightness of touch when used in the daytime.

The fireplace shows the intricate detailing of Webb's fretwork on the panelling and provides a stunning focal point in the room. It's the same colour as the rest of the room, but the small unpainted wooden shelves on each side provide contrast for the display of favourite objects. The gilt-framed pictures add glamour and sparkle, especially when catching the lamplight in the evenings.

The woven wool curtains and chair covers are both in the 'Peacock and Dragon' design by William Morris. Created with natural dyes, some of these textiles have faded over time, but they still show the stunning effect you can achieve with textured patterned fabrics in co-ordinated colours, and the way they can pull together the colours from the rest of the decorative scheme.

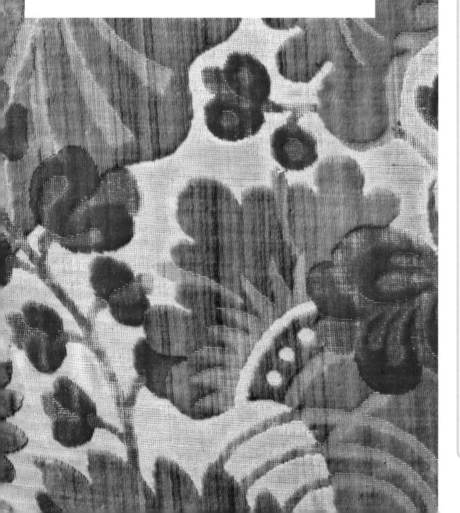

green and red

Green and red are contrasting colours and can create exciting and dynamic schemes. Success lies in not allowing the two colours to compete, so try one as the main colour and use the other more sparingly. Another solution is to use softer shades of both.

a touch of green

A collection of green paperweights catches the light and draws the eye to a corner of the drawing room at Antony.

A favourite painting or framed print (such as *Girl with a Violin* by Henry Harewood Robinson at Lanhydrock) can be all you need to bring a gentle shade of green into your room.

Above: This elegant bedroom at Wimpole Hall brings together restful shades of green for the walls and reddish-pink for the bed drapes and headboard. The floral green-and-pink chintz sofa and curtains embody the country-house look.

Left: Sofas in a soft leaf-green make an attractive combination with the bold red ceiling lamps and patterned carpet at Chatham holiday cottage. Touches of black in the light fittings and gold motifs on the shades have given the scheme a dash of glamour.

the 'wow' factor

The Arts and Crafts period saw some sensational designs for wallpaper. For its flamboyant use of green and adventurous full-on pattern, this bedroom at Wightwick Manor is hard to beat.

The 'Acanthus' design by William Morris is bold, but when used on some of the sloping walls and accentuated by the dark wood picture rail, it has extra impact. The vivid emerald-green carpet adds to the luxurious effect but the white-painted ceiling and cream cover on the bed have given the room some fresh touches and prevented it from becoming overwhelming.

Botanical and other nature-inspired wallpaper designs make a great choice for any room – but always try out large samples at home first to be sure the designs you're considering suit the size and scale of your room.

yellow

Mustard or saffron, lemon or maize, the yellow palette can bring an uplifting and cheerful feel to a room.

- Yellow ochre, an earth pigment, has been used as a paint since prehistoric times.
- Lemon yellow was fashionable in the Regency era and was a favourite of the architect Sir John Soane, who used it in his own home in Lincoln's Inn Fields.
- In 1809 an artificial 'chrome yellow' was discovered, extracted from the mineral crocoite by French chemist Louis Vauquelin.
- The German writer Goethe, whose many published works included *Theory of Colours*, believed that 'yellow makes a thoroughly warm and comforting impression'.
- Primrose yellow was a popular colour in Edwardian interiors and heralded a move away from the darker palette of late Victorian decoration towards lighter schemes.

Right: The spectacular drawing room designed by Sir John Soane for Wimpole Hall.

Below: Rococo carved ceiling with a lemon yellow, white and pistachio colour scheme at Claydon House.

Left: At the turn of the 20th century, society hostess Mrs Ronnie Greville chose a sunny yellow for her study at Polesden Lacey.

yellow schemes

Yellow is bright and cheerful and can be very energising, so consider restricting it to paler shades in rooms where you want to relax.

Yellow and black create schemes with impact. At Hinton Ampner (above left) a bright and cheerful yellow for walls and upholstery is contrasted with touches of black from the decorative side tables.

At Castle Drogo the bathroom tiles (above) show the stylish mix of black decorative motifs on a yellow background.

shades of yellow

Try soft primrose yellow with touches of jade and cream for a breezy seaside feel, teamed with checked fabrics and fresh whitewashed furniture.

For refined elegance, use muted yellow ochre and terracotta with touches of olive, natural-fibre rugs and faded chintz.

Pep up pale and lemon yellow with zesty hints of lime or orange.

Mustard yellow with splashes of turquoise and aqua make a smart team alongside white woodwork and oak furniture.

Boost the effect of all yellows by adding fresh white on doors, mouldings and accessories.

Bring sophisticated chic to yellow by combining it with soft greys, lilac and pearl white.

Bright yellow curtains and William Morris 'Pomegranate' wallpaper with its accents of red have created an exuberant bedroom scheme at Cragside (above). However, the oak furniture, and white paintwork and ceiling have prevented the final effect from becoming too powerful.

The hall and staircase at the Arts and Crafts house, Standen (above) show how touches of other colours can boost the effect of a yellow-and-white decorative scheme. The turquoise vases on the half-landing and the sunflower and blue jugs further up the stairs provide an eye-catching contrast to the William Morris wallpaper.

easy elegance

A room doesn't have to be full of bold colours or patterns to make an impact. Tranquil hues and coordinating accessories can help you create a stylish scheme.

Yellow and blue are a winning combination. This pretty bedroom at Melford Hall has been decorated in pale creamy yellow for the walls and a yellow silk for the bed hangings.

Soft blues on chairs, bed trimming and tie-backs are echoed in the patterned rug and floral curtains.

The celebrated 20th-century interior decorator John Fowler designed this drawing room at Fenton House in his signature country-house style (above). Two shades of yellow were used on the walls, with the lighter hue inside the mouldings. Floral chintz upholstery unites the yellow walls and red and green chairs.

At Anglesey Abbey (above), the walls and carpet have wedded two lively colours with exciting results. It's not overpowering because the creamy yellow walls are muted, allowing the strong purple carpet to emerge as the star player. An opulent Rococo-style headboard and the patterned bed cover ties the colour scheme together.

a touch of yellow

A framed print of lemons against a black background will give a colourful zing to any room (above).

A single chair in a yellow-striped fabric will pep up a dark corner (left).

For a 1950s retro look, display yellow and blue china against a primrose wall (below).

the 'wow' factor

Print rooms were a popular way to embellish interiors in the 18th century, created by pasting engravings and prints on to the walls to give the illusion of a gallery of framed pictures. This was a pastime enjoyed by both men and women and, as the trend grew, manufacturers began producing sets of paper prints, borders and bows.

This enchanting decorative scheme at Uppark is an exquisite example of a print room. The prints shown here are on a yellow background – a typical colour for print rooms – and combined with white woodwork they show what a gorgeous look it can offer. If you fancy adding a little Georgian flair to your home this is a surprisingly easy look to emulate.

All you need to do is photocopy pictures and prints (you can stain them with tea to achieve an 'aged' appearance) and paste them to the wall. Stencils can be used to create the frames and bow effects, but you can also buy ready-made paper swags and ribbons for all the finishing touches. Print-room-effect wallpapers are also available for those who love the look but prefer a simpler option.

orange

Orange can bring a warm glow to any scheme. It is a strong colour to use on its own and tends to work best when applied in small amounts, or as an accent colour. However, orange also comes in many softer colours such as peach and apricot and warm, spicy tones, so experiment with a shade that works for you.

Left: Orange and red crockery make a vivid display in the kitchen at Scotney Castle.

Above left: Tangerine-coloured cupboard doors give a sharp citrus accent to the kitchen at Little Chert holiday cottage. The roller blind in orange with other bright colours adds even more zest.

Above: A single orange chair in a neutral scheme at The Homewood makes a striking focal point and warms a cold area.

red

The red palette includes ruby and scarlet, cranberry and wine, and can bring warmth, drama and energy to a scheme.

- Red dyes for early textiles came from vegetation such as the root of the madder plant (*Rubia tinctorum*).
- Expensive jewel-coloured red was extracted from the insects kermes and cochineal.
- The walls of many picture rooms were decorated in red as it was considered to be the best background for the display of gilt-framed paintings.
- Traditionally, iron oxide was used to produce an earthy pale pink.
- A terracotta 'Pompeian red' became popular in the 18th century after the discovery of Roman ruins revealed evidence of red decoration.

Left: The crimson bedroom at Basildon Park is a bold, confident scheme.

Right: Vivid red features in the floral Réveillon wallpaper is combined with the silk-upholstered pink chairs at Clandon Park.

red schemes

Red is a colour that can invigorate a room so choose it when you want to bring energy and excitement to a space.

Ernö Goldfinger used primary colours as part of his Modernist scheme at 2 Willow Road. A glossy red door and chair creates a bold feature in the hallway against the blue wall (left). White used on the other wall adds freshness and contrast. Red and white walls also create blocks of colour in the dining room (right).

Shades of red

Burgundy and rich, deep wine shades work well with red-patterned carpets and dark wood furniture and create an opulent atmosphere.

Red checked and striped fabrics will bring a smart touch to a crisp white or cream scheme.

Scarlet red with touches of gold will pack a glamorous punch in any room.

Ruby red complements dove grey, and brings an air of sophistication to any setting.

red and white

Red is warm and dramatic and can spice up any room. It is an ideal partner for white, which will bring freshness to the scheme.

Scarlet walls bring a rich atmosphere to the elegant living room at Plas Newydd (above). The scheme has been enlivened by white used for the fire-surround and the panelling below the dado rail. Further contrast comes from the white decorative frieze.

The original Victorian colour scheme for the hall at Standen was blood red, but the family found it too gloomy. With it repainted in white, touches of red introduced through the velvet chairs becomes accent colour rather than the main element (above).

An eye-catching feature has been made of the doors at Coughton Court (above) by painting them red with mouldings picked out in white. If you're unsure about using red in quantity, this is an idea for injecting a little colour into a room, while keeping the rest of your décor more neutral.

A lively mix of red and white has been achieved through a careful choice of red curtains, rug and upholstery at The Dairy House holiday cottage (above). The neutral carpet and white walls keep the whole look bright and modern.

exciting combinations

**Red combined with other bold colours
can create a luxurious atmosphere.**

No other colour combination has quite the excitement of red
and black, as the Mary Queen of Scots bedroom at Hardwick
Hall illustrates (above). Even without the sumptuous drapes,
a red headboard and black-patterned bedcover would add
thrilling impact to any bedroom.

Elegant pale blue walls have softened the effect of blood-red
curtains and carpet to offer an appealing and stylish colour
pairing at Lanhydrock (above). The dark wood panelling and
staircase look equally good against both colours and have
united the scheme.

Decorative touches of gold on the bedcover, its drapes and around the walls have added flair to a theatrical-looking red bedroom at Castle Coole (below). Swathes of white muslin could also be used for bed drapes to create a similar but softer effect.

Red becomes a smart companion to cream in a sophisticated scheme at Odcombe holiday cottage (below). Decorative fringing on the curtains and cushion complete this chic look.

pink

Today, pink is associated with girls' bedrooms and ultra-feminine schemes, but the pink palette is remarkably varied. From hot fuchsia to dusky terracotta, pink offers a wealth of decorative choice with effects ranging from the dramatic and invigorating to the tranquil and serene.

A touch of pink

A simple display of freshly cut roses in a white jug is all that's needed to bring a subtle hint of pink to a room.

Decorative as well as useful, hat boxes in pink and cream will add a stylish touch to a bedroom.

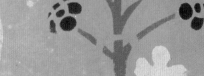

pink and white

If you think a pink-and-white decorative scheme might be a bit too sugary, the enchanting drawing room at Greys Court may persuade you to give it a try.

The drawing room (below) is both refined and relaxed, with its comfortable sofas, floral upholstery and time-worn rug. While the pink-and-white décor gives the room a wedding-cake prettiness, this is tempered by sophisticated accessories and furnishings and brighter pink cushions.

This decorative scheme makes the most of the plentiful light from the large windows all around the room, enhanced by curtain treatments, simple and elegant in neutral cream linen. The co-ordinating shell-shaped pelmets and smart trimmings add a chic touch.

Greys Court has retained its exquisite 18th-century Rococo plasterwork, where the intricate details have been highlighted in white to stand out against the pink background. But plaster details, dado rails, and decorative mouldings of all styles would look just as good painted white against walls in other pale or pastel colours, such as sky blue, dove grey or primrose yellow.

pink schemes

Traditional or modern interiors will respond well to pink if you choose the right shade. Depending on the other colours you use, the results can be uplifting or restful.

A little black will make a pink scheme 'pop' and adds a touch of sophistication. The black-and-white floor at Portland House holiday cottage (above) enlivens the candy pink bathroom.

A tranquil atmosphere has been created at Dunkery View holiday cottage (above) with delicate shell-pink walls and white-painted beams. Simple pine furniture adds to the homely cottage charm.

The epitome of relaxed country-house style, the kitchen at Greys Court includes pink-painted furniture teamed with cheerful floral fabrics (right).

pink shades

**Different rooms show
the wide variety of pinks
available for home décor.**

This 1930s decorative scheme for a bedroom at Plas Newydd (left) was the work of Sybil Colefax of Colefax and Fowler. It is feminine with softly flowing pink curtains and dressing-table drapery. However, a bolder pink for the lampshades and the green and pink floral chintz on the sofa have given the room a sophisticated edge.

Hot pink and black have produced extraordinary, bold effects in a bathroom at Basildon Park (above). Its exuberance adds impact to a small room, but a less lively effect could be achieved by using towels and accessories in these colours against neutral décor.

the 'wow' factor

Who could resist the Hollywood-style glamour of this fabulous bedroom at Wimpole Hall?

Sophisticated and elegant, the sumptuous swags and drapes on the bed are of crimson brocade covered in lace, producing a delicious pinky red. The elaborate white-and-gold bed frame, and the rich red curtains and rugs, complete a scheme that is pure theatre.

Pink and red can be a successful and exciting colour combination that will result in amazing room schemes. Success often lies in the contrast, so try using strong, bright red with a soft pastel pink. Use them together as striped curtains or upholstery, or with one as the main colour, such as pale pink walls with the red as an accent shade for cushions or lampshades.

black

Black has a role to play in any scheme where you wish to inject drama or sophistication.

- Sources of the earliest black pigments included charcoal.
- Roman mosaic floors included intricate black-and-white geometric patterns.
- Schemes in black and white were popular in the Art Deco period, evocative of Hollywood glamour.
- Some Modernist architects used black in their schemes alongside chrome, glass and polished wood.

Left: Silhouettes make a striking feature, such as this of scientist Otto Overbeck at Overbeck's.

Above: Transfer-printed Liverpool fireplace tiles at Croft Castle show how effective black and white can be together.

Above: An elaborate silver tap makes a strong style statement against the black marble splashback in Lady Iliffe's bathroom at Basildon Park.

black schemes

Black is dramatic and eye-catching and even the smallest amount can pep up a room.

using black

Try black as an accent colour for piping on coloured cushions or as tie-backs to cream-coloured curtains.

Team black and white for strong contrast – a classic combination for chequerboard-tiled floors and walls.

Black with gold or silver is the ultimate in glamour – try a feature wall in shimmering metallic-coated black-patterned wallpaper or a wall of black tiles in a bathroom.

For a chic modern look, add touches of black to a coffee-and-cream colour scheme or to give pastels a lift.

At Hinton Ampner, black has been used in the bath alcove to add flair and a Hollywood feel (above left). Fresh white towels and other accessories give the scheme a crisp look.

A few touches of black have added interest to a bathroom at Anglesey Abbey (above), especially through the band of black marble around the bottom of the walls. A decorative black sculpture adds an extra stylish twist.

focus on black and white

This Art Deco bedroom at Coleton Fishacre was designed for Lady Dorothy D'Oyly Carte, daughter-in-law of the famed impresario who first staged Gilbert and Sullivan's comic operas. Here we see a lively mix of bold colour and monochrome pattern, in true Deco style.

Among the highlights in the room are the black-and-white linen curtains and cushions, created by painter and designer Raoul Dufy. The dressing-table stool is the original, and although the curtains are reproductions – they were done by the same French firm that made the textiles in the 1920s.

The room is a dynamic mix, with the strong black-and-white elements complemented by the dark blue of the carpet and a deep purple-red on the quilted bedspreads. However, the walls have been kept a simple white and the chair covers are in a neutral shade. These, together with the pale limed-oak furniture, tone down the richer hues, and the overall feel is 'smart casual'.

Loose covers are practical and have a relaxed look to them. They're a great way to change the appearance and mood of a room without the expense of new furniture. The neutral colours don't compete with the busy pattern in the room, and the black piping and cushions tie them all into a co-ordinated look.

An extra colour has been introduced to the room with the jewel-coloured red bed covers, which can be turned down during the day or left covering the whole bed for added impact. Other colours would work equally well but would create a different mood: a white or cream bedspread would give the room less colour contrast and a more serene feel, while a further flourish might be achieved with bed covers or cushions in the same pattern as the curtains.

a dash of black

Accents of black can bring extra depth to your decorative schemes, especially those that include warm colours such as orange and red.

At Ivy Cottage holiday house, a Victorian-style brass bed is embellished with black, red and silver detailing (below left). The red bedside lamps add to the richness of the scheme.

The striking mix of black, white and red have transformed a bathroom at Vyner holiday cottage into a deliciously indulgent space (below right). The gilt-framed mirror over the basin adds richness and sparkle.

Colour has been used to define different spaces for sleeping, eating and relaxing in an open-plan living arrangement at Little Chert holiday cottage (right). The black footstool makes a bold contrast to the glass table and chairs and bright orange tablerunner. Pure white for the bedroom area, with a dash of black detailing and a sea-blue rug, lends an air of calm and repose.

stylish touches

Objects and pictures in black, or black and white, make a great display against a neutral backdrop.

Below: The smallest touches of black can bring style to a neutral wall, exemplified by this black mosaic-patterned clock at Greenway.

Right: The Ancient and Classical worlds unite – a striking black sphinx ornament stands out against a white wall and elegant marble fireplace at Mottisfont.

Opposite: Frame a set of black-and-white architectural prints or photographs to bring a smart touch to a room.

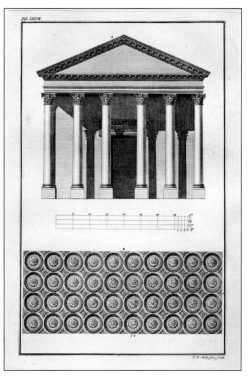

the 'wow' factor

At Lanhydrock, a striking and opulent bedroom is created by the black-and-gold patterned wallpaper, a copy of an original design by Augustus Pugin for the House of Lords.

Wallpapers are enjoying a comeback and there are some spectacular Gothic and medieval-style patterns available to achieve this luxurious look.

The half-tester mahogany bed with brown-fringed drapes is a strong focal point and shows how well black and gold work together with rich wood furniture. The white cover on the bed lightens the look and helps to keep the decorative scheme comfortable and not too intense. Additional notes of black come from the rug and the fireplace.

white and neutrals

The neutral palette includes cream and beige, chocolate and tan, and complements a wide variety of classic and modern schemes.

- For centuries, walls were whitened with lime-wash and chalk distemper.
- Stone was a popular shade for Georgian hallways and stone itself could be faked with *trompe l'oeil* wallpapers.
- In the 1920s, interior decorator Syrie Maugham set a trend for rooms decorated entirely in different hues of white.
- White decorative plasterwork was often embellished with gilding, especially in Neo-classical interiors.

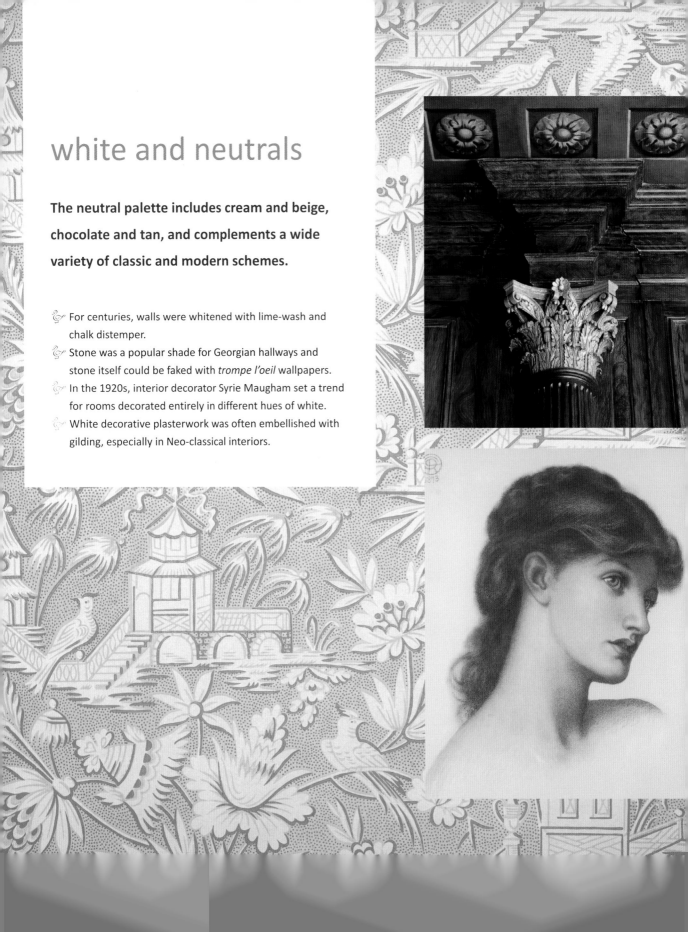

Above left: The rich brown scheme at Hanbury Hall includes a *trompe l'oeil* ceiling.

Left: *Bust of a Woman Turned to the Right* by Dante Gabriel Rossetti hangs at Wightwick Manor.

Right: The elaborate plasterwork ceiling and frieze, and the oak panelling create a strong backdrop to the patterned floor at Buckland Abbey.

white and
neutral schemes

Rooms in these colours are tranquil and understated. Just add a few colour contrasts for interest.

using neutrals

Choose materials with different textures such as glass, mirror, wood, linen and wool to give neutral schemes interest and prevent them looking bland.

Try cream or soft white and touches of dove grey with faded floral fabrics for an elegant look.

For white or neutral kitchens, add splashes of bright colour with blue, red or orange accessories.

For a smart and sophisticated look combine shades of cream, coffee and chocolate for curtains, upholstery and cushions.

Add a dash of black to any neutral scheme for dramatic impact.

Far left: An enchanting pairing of white with coffee-coloured shades at Nostell Priory.

Left: Neutral colours and some clever design have turned an awkward, narrow space into a practical, stylish bathroom at the Round House holiday cottage.

Below: Serene neutral shades have enhanced a tranquil bedroom at Ightham Mote. The goose-wing grey walls with mouldings picked out in white are a perfect combination with armchairs upholstered in soft pink.

Below left: Neutral shades add interest to the corner of the study at The Homewood.

Left: A corner of the drawing room at Red House with its painted panelling has created a restful spot to relax, enlivened by gentle colours in the embroidered cushions and window seat.

neutral backdrops

Successful neutral schemes can allow accents of other colours to create different moods and looks.

A chic country-house style is achieved with a neutral backdrop in one of the bedrooms at Shute Barton holiday cottage (left). Key to the look are the dark wood bed frame, ornate dressing-table and other pieces of antique furniture which make a strong statement without the need for colourful surroundings. Touches of muted colour in the gold-and-red patterned curtains and rug complement the scheme.

At Housesteads holiday cottage (above), the splashes of colour from the roller blinds and seat cushions in the kitchen give a lift to a pretty, neutral palette of cream walls, natural stone and wood. Soft furnishings can easily be changed and updated when required to create a new look.

neutral but rich

Bring added interest to a scheme by combining textures and decorative accessories in co-ordinating shades from the neutral palette.

At the Homewood a rich blend of chocolate-brown walls, a pale wood floor, white vinyl chairs and a tinted glass dining-table creates a look that is sophisticated yet effortlessly relaxed (right). Although modern, the look works superbly with antique touches from the historic portraits on the wall.

A decorative and ornate cornice picked out in gold is a bold contrast to the neutral backdrop in the morning room at Mottisfont (above). The cream walls and pale carpet create a soothing and restful setting, allowing the books, pictures and sofa to provide splashes of colour.

A stencil decoration around the top of the wall would achieve a similar effect in a room without original cornicing or architectural details.

The hallway at Monk's House (above) shows that neutral schemes can still be full of interest, with its mix of beige and cream and dark and light woods. The star of the show is the patterned canvaswork mirror frame, which combines the colours of the natural shades around it and reflected opposite. The fluted column, well-worn tiled floor and rough wood of the ceiling beam add textural contrast.

focus on neutrals

Neutral schemes don't get more stylish than this sophisticated and versatile open-plan living-room at The Homewood. Designed by Modernist architect Patrick Gwynne in the 1930s, it includes later items of furniture which he added to update the rooms. This light, airy and uncluttered style is still eminently popular and practical for today's lifestyles.

With subtle colours and big picture windows, the scheme creates a restful haven as well as a fusion of indoors and out. Here, it is the placement of furniture and rugs which subdivides the different areas of the open-plan space. Fabulous folding-screen doors have also been used to open up – or divide – the living-room and the adjoining dining area when required.

One of the many successful elements of the room is the combination of textures – an important factor for largely neutral settings, adding interest and variation. Smooth glass, gleaming marble and polished wood floors combine with the weave and deep pile of cream wool rugs and the undulating forms of the chair and footstool.

Folding screens and doors were a feature of Modernist houses. This one was designed as a sliding 'wall', but free-standing screens are another option if you want to divide up a large room. Here, a different design has been used for each side, one with images of bamboo in greys and white, the other depicting gold stalks of sweetcorn, stark and bold against a black background.

The success of the largely neutral bedroom scheme at Shute Barton holiday cottage (above) comes from plenty of textural interest, such as the coarse-weave beige carpet and patterned rug providing contrast with the smooth wooden bed and leather chair. The white paint on the mouldings and cornice accentuate the architectural interest of the room. A combination of curtains and smart roller blinds has added variety.

A rustic, cottage style is achieved in one of the bathrooms at Wightwick Manor (above). Different shades of cream, white and brown have been combined with contrasting black-painted wooden floorboards and a textured mat, resulting in a scheme that is full of interest. The pretty washstand and painted chest of drawers add extra charm.

The streamlined good looks of The Homewood are enhanced by a combination of textures in a neutral scheme (above). The pale wall covering blends with the smooth wood of the bookshelf and side tables, while the mushroom-brown bedcover and cream leather bed frame add to the simplicity of the room.

An irresistible bedroom scheme at Tredegar House (above) owes much of its success to a rich combination of textures and neutral shades. The sumptuous dark brown and gold-patterned curtains have been allowed to pool on to the pale carpet, while the mouldings have been picked out in white against the dove-grey panelled walls.

neutral details

Make the most of neutral schemes with decorative displays and accessories.

Intricate metal scrollwork has transformed a plain glazed door in a neutral hallway into something rather Rococo-esque at the Hardmans' House (above).

A straw hat perched casually atop a plaster bust makes a quirky focal point in the neutral entrance hall at Greenway (above). It is unexpected combinations like this which will draw the eye.

Texture adds interest to neutral schemes, especially through objects and accessories for display. An elegant cut-glass decanter against the cream beading of the wall makes a pleasing contrast to faded leather books (above).

the 'wow' factor

Layers of texture have created a room brimming with interest in this neutral but glamorous bedroom at Nunnington Hall. Richly patterned textiles as wall hangings, piles of plump cushions as accessories, and the wooden four-poster bed with its drapery are the key ingredients that have added weight and depth to the scheme.

The off-white painted walls have drawn attention to the architectural details of the woodwork and panelling and small touches of colour from the rugs, pictures and the painted bed footboard have kept the effect cosy and welcoming.

Try layering up a neutral bedroom scheme with favourite rugs, cushions and throws, and even a tapestry or embroidered wall hanging for an elegant but relaxing feel.

pattern

pattern

Pattern has embellished homes throughout history and reflected many changes in fashion and taste. Decorative designs have made their way on to every surface, including carpets, furniture, wallpapers, fabrics, plasterwork and countless forms of ceramic art.

Some patterns have become synonymous with certain periods or great names, such as the patterned stained glass in Victorian homes, the exotic glazed tiles of William de Morgan and the swirls and geometric shapes of Art Deco.

While patterns may be complex – our ancestors weren't shy when it came to applying them liberally – they may also be subtle and used with restraint, so the scope for using them in the home is enormous. Whether a pattern stands alone, setting the whole scene, or offers a supporting role in the form of finishing touches, it can bring any decorative scheme to life.

Left: Detail of 'peacock' wallpaper at Erddig.

Above: A pretty floral rug and curtains add a feminine feel at Llanerchaeron.

Above right: At Trerice, tile-effect wallpaper has been used around the walls of a bathroom.

using pattern

Before you buy a patterned wallpaper or fabric, obtain the largest samples you can in order to see how they will look in your room.

Many manufacturers offer ranges of mix-and-match patterns which will help you achieve a co-ordinated look.

If you are unsure about patterned wallpaper for a whole room, try it as a feature on one wall and keep the others plain. The wall behind the bed makes a great focal point.

Create an elegant period feel with patterned wallpaper above a dado rail and a matching plain colour for the wall beneath.

As a general rule, vertical lines and stripes will draw the eye upwards and can make a low ceiling seem higher, while horizontal lines can make a narrow room seem wider.

One large pattern mixed with smaller ones in the same colour palette can be a harmonious combination.

Consider the size of your room when you are choosing pattern. Some strong, large patterns might overwhelm a small space, while a tiny or delicate design may be lost in a big room.

Think about how collections or pictures will look against patterned wallpaper – you don't want them to compete.

patterned schemes

Four attractive rooms illustrate how patterns can be used to create cosy and inviting spaces.

A bedroom is our personal space, and offers the chance to indulge our creative impulses. In the honeysuckle bedroom at Wightwick Manor (above), layers of rich pattern have resulted in a warm and alluring retreat, with sumptuous wallpaper and rugs cleverly combined with delicately embroidered bed hangings. The white-painted ceiling and skirting boards lift the scheme and give it a freshness so that the result is not too overpowering.

Pattern makes a bold statement, as this bathroom at Lanhydrock illustrates (above). The grand roll-top bath is teamed with elegant washstands and basins for a luxurious effect, but the real star of the room is the fabulous lilac patterned wallpaper, which creates a dramatic and faintly exotic backdrop to the whole spectacular scheme.

Arts and Crafts houses reveal clever combinations of plain panelling with patterned wallpaper. At Standen (above), the colourful 'Fruit' wallpaper by Morris is balanced by the fresh white-painted panelling below.

At Wightwick Manor (above) a wallpaper design by J.H. Dearle has been used above dark wood panelling. Notice how the pictures on the wall, with their wide mounts and simple matching frames, complement the wallpaper rather than compete with it.

flower power

Floral patterns are among the most popular designs and people have used them for generations to bring style to their country homes and townhouses.

Decorative flowers can be seen in surviving Egyptian murals and Roman frescoes, and in the interiors and artefacts of ancient cultures across the world. They recur as motifs for tapestries, embroideries, wood carvings, marquetry, furniture and ceramics throughout the ages.

Fresh flowers also enjoyed an important place in the home as lavish arrangements for dinner parties or flamboyant displays in hallways. When tulips first arrived in Britain in the 17th century, houses such as Dyrham Park were among those to show these blooms in newly fashionable blue-and-white Delft vases.

Throughout the 20th century, when Modernism and geometric designs were making their mark, floral patterns kept their appeal. Renowned interior decorator John Fowler enhanced the glamour and nostalgia of flowers when he co-founded the design firm Colefax and Fowler.

Far Left: One of the most cheerful and welcoming of all historic houses must be George Bernard Shaw's former home, Shaw's Corner. Here, the simple decorative scheme in the sunny dual-aspect living-room contributes to its charm, with cream walls and woodwork complementing the restful floral upholstery and curtains.

Left: In the 18th century it became fashionable to use the same pattern or design for curtains and upholstery to create a co-ordinated look. At Antony, a delightfully tranquil bedroom has been created with a single floral pattern set against soft blue-green painted panelled walls, the whole enhanced by an elegant yet simple neutral carpet.

Above: A bright red carpet has made the floral patterns burst into life at Dunham Massey and picks out the shades in the upholstery and curtains. The painted panelling and mouldings have given texture to the scheme, and form a subtle backdrop to the bolder pattern and colour.

focus on florals

Antony is the epitome of the elegant and welcoming country house. Built in the 18th century by Sir William Carew, it is still the family's home. Among its stunning interiors is the south bedroom, a serene and unashamedly romantic space, decorated and refurnished in 1950. Fully panelled, and painted in a pale dusky blue, the walls are a tranquil backdrop to the pretty floral upholstery and soft furnishings.

The patterns and textures work effortlessly together, from the alternating plain and floral panels of the bed hangings to the antique rugs and raspberry-pink carpet. The blue-and-white tiled fireplace also adds a delicate note of colour and light. The undoubted star piece, however, is the Georgian mahogany four-poster bed, with its carved and gilded cresting.

Floral chintz is a timeless country classic and here the delicate pinks are enhanced by the addition of pink lacy cushions. Designs such as this suit a variety of traditional interiors, but don't worry if you have a modern house – florals work perfectly in contemporary settings too. Some fabric companies produce prints from period archives, while others have reworked them to create patterns with an edgy modern twist.

Individual display objects can become key players in a decorative scheme. This pretty porcelain dish picks up not only the pinks and greens in the fabrics and the gold of the bed and picture frames, but also the creams in the lampshades. If you're looking for inspiration, a favourite piece like this can be as much the starting point for a colour scheme as the finishing touch.

tapestry treasures

From medieval times tapestries provided pattern and decoration, serving as wall hangings, curtains around four-poster beds and table coverings. As well as having a practical use against draughts, they could also be taken down and transported whenever the owner travelled.

The product of highly skilled weavers, tapestries were expensive, and became a status symbol of luxury and wealth. Bess of Hardwick, one of the most powerful women in Elizabethan England, accumulated a fabulous range of tapestries and embroideries depicting biblical scenes, animals and plants to display in Hardwick Hall, her splendid home in Derbyshire.

The popularity of tapestries as wall-hangings began to wane in the late 18th century with the rise in demand for wall panelling and surge of interest in wallpapers and stencilled designs, but

they enjoyed a renaissance with the Victorians and especially the Arts and Crafts designers, led by William Morris. Ironically, although he designed more than 50 wallpapers, Morris preferred textile hangings for his own homes.

Patterned tapestries and embroideries are available today in a wide variety of styles as wall-hangings but also for cushions, upholstered footstools, chairs and other furniture. Some are replicas of early originals with medieval imagery, while others are new designs in bold contemporary colours and patterns.

Above Left: A tapestry design by Edward Burne-Jones and William Morris at Wightwick Manor.

Above: A traditional tapestry hangs in Retainer's Court holiday cottage as the main focus for the room, adding a striking period touch but also creating a clever alternative to a headboard.

Above: The holiday apartment at Standen is part of the original Arts and Crafts house but has been decorated with a more modern twist. Patterned wall hangings add texture and colour, with their tones echoed in matching cushions; all sit happily alongside new furniture.

birds, butterflies and chinoiserie

Between the late 17th and early 19th centuries there was a tate for exotic styles from Asia. Home owners were keen to show off their flair and use decorative elements in their interiors. Among the most popular were Chinese wallpapers.

Imported by the East India Company, these wallpapers were often hand painted with images of flowering trees, landscapes, butterflies, birds and scenes of rural life. Some papers were also coated with mica to produce a shimmering finish.

Chinese wallpaper was a favourite of many architects and designers and was used frequently in bedroom settings. Nostell Priory in Yorkshire contains the stunning Chinese papers supplied and hung in 1771 by Thomas Chippendale. Today's revival of interest in patterned wallpapers has created a wealth of choice if you're looking for similar designs to the Far Eastern papers of the past. They range from bespoke hand-painted and replica papers to high-street collections which take inspiration from the originals but have a contemporary feel.

toile de Jouy

As a design classic, *toile de Jouy* lends a chic note to contemporary schemes as much as it does to elegant period interiors. It takes its name from the town of Jouy-en-Josas in France, where production began in the 1760s. Plain cottons or linens were printed in one colour, very often pink, with romantic pastoral scenes, flowers, trees and classical imagery.

Toile often works best when the same pattern and colour is used throughout a room. This bedroom at Deer Park holiday cottage has a pretty pale blue *toile* for the bed cover and curtains, but its charm has been accentuated by applying it to the panels on the wardrobe doors. An extra smart touch is the navy braid around the edge of each panel, also used on the curtains.

painted decoration

**Over the generations home owners have
sought to mimic more expensive materials
through clever paint effects, and in the 17th
and 18th centuries house painters became
skilled at producing imitations of exotic
woods, leather and textiles.**

Schemes also included stencilled patterns, incredible *trompe
l'oeil* illusions and marbling, the latter being a popular effect
for a variety of different surfaces including walls, fire-
surrounds and columns.

Historic houses offer a treasure trove of inspiring paint effects
and patterns which can act as the starting point for a decorative
scheme. Depending on your artistic ability, these can be copied
freehand or stencilled, or you can choose from ranges of
ready-to-use paper borders or effects.

Stencilling has enjoyed a long history. At medieval Bradley
(above left), a fleur-de-lis motif transformed the white walls.
If you don't want to use stencils across a whole wall like this,
try them as a border around the ceiling.

Attingham Park's beautiful boudoir (above) glows with
its painted wall decorations, depicting scrolls, flowers and
ribbons. One or two of these motifs from a stencil could be
used to bring similar elegant pattern to a room.

A rich marbling effect has given depth and interest to the wood panelling below a tapestry border at Belton House (above). Short courses that teach the art of marbling, wood graining and other effects offer a great way to try your hand at these skills.

Take a lead from William Morris and have a go at creating your own decorative border or frieze around the room. The detail above right shows his design of flowers and scrolling ribbons for the drawing room at Red House, discovered under later panelling. The inscription in French reads '*Qui bien aime tard oublie*' ('Who loves well forgets slowly').

Baroque style

The Restoration of Charles II saw a profusion of decorative murals and paintings. They were a key element of the Baroque style, which started in around 1600 in Rome, which offered sumptuous decoration and jaw-dropping theatrical results, particularly effective on huge staircases, ceilings and in public reception rooms.

take two stripes

Stripes have a lasting appeal. They can be used effectively in traditional or modern homes as the basis of a whole decorative scheme or for just a few accessories.

Bold blue stripes in a sunburst effect on the rug at Little Chert holiday cottage (left) make a bold contrast to the orange accents.

The power of stripes can be seen in one of the bedrooms at Godolphin holiday cottage (above). The bed cover is the only pattern needed in the decoration of this tranquil interior, where hints of the blue are echoed in the colour-washed wood-panelled walls behind the bed.

the 'wow' factor

The early 19th century saw a fashion for rooms draped with fabric, which mimicked Napoleonic campaign tents and motifs and followed the style set by the Empress Josephine at the Château de Malmaison, near Paris.

This 'tented' bedroom scheme at Kingston Lacy was created by the Bankes family in the 1830s, with paint effects including swags and rope tassels on the walls and striped paper on the ceiling. Even the bed valance is a matching fabric.

This idea would work especially well in attic rooms with sloping eaves, which lend themselves to the tent style. If you choose not to try real fabric to create the effect, there are striped wallpapers and ready-made paper tassels, swags and rope motifs available to help achieve the look.

texture

texture

As texture communicates the feel or appearance of a surface, it's an important part of adding visual interest to a room scheme, especially when different textures are combined – think of the pleasing effect created by smooth wood and glass combined with woven textiles and deep-pile carpets and rugs.

Texture is especially important in single-colour and neutral schemes as it prevents the effect appearing dull and flat. In a cream and white room, for example, depth and interest can be created by a carved wooden table next to a linen sofa with an embroidered throw or cushions.

From the earliest times natural flooring added texture to the home. Thick fibres from plants such as bulrush were plaited and sewn together to make mats, which could then be laid over stone or wooden floors. Rich and poor alike used them and many varieties are still made today, including designs from coir, seagrass and sisal.

Hard flooring brought texture indoors too, from the rough-hewn flagstones of humble homes to the gleaming marble and inlaid wooden floors of the rich. Tapestry hangings and panelled walls also added rich texture to rooms, along with the different weaves of damask, linen and wool used for bed drapes, blankets and cushions.

Above: Floor-to-ceiling painted panelling has provided a deep textured backdrop to a cosy bedroom scheme at Erddig.

Right and far right: The textured carpet in the saloon at Coleton Fishacre makes an unusual but dramatic centrepiece.

A clever use of texture can be seen at Coleton Fishacre, in the geometric deep-pile carpet by renowned Art Deco designer Marion Dorn. This and the rough plaster walls make a strong contrast to the smooth, reflective surfaces of chrome, mirror-topped side tables and the marble chimney piece.

With space only for a bed, a narrow room at Cotehele (above) becomes an inviting retreat thanks to the textured tapestry wall hangings, patterned bed cover and rug.

If you fancy a simpler alternative, why not choose a cream embroidered quilt or bedcover to add textural interest to your room?

Highly textured rush matting provides the starting point for an informal but striking scheme at Chartwell (above). The natural fibres blend with the botanical-themed chair covers and plain green curtains to create a fresh garden-room feel.

A chair at Castle Drogo has been partly upholstered in a richly patterned carpet-style design, with additional impact from the thickly textured decorative fringe (above).

A bold-coloured cover on an occasional table adds rich texture to the corner of the writing room at Sissinghurst Castle (above) and complements the tactile qualities of the ornaments and plant pot.

a cosy retreat

A variety of interesting textures and lively patterns will enrich any scheme, especially when combined with atmospheric lighting.

At 575 Wandsworth Road, poet Khadambi Asalache created a remarkable home with his hand-carved fretwork and decorative painting, drawing inspiration from a variety of cultural sources to produce his own unique style. Here in the living room, the fretwork backdrop is augmented by layers of pattern and texture from cushions, kilims and the striking textile wall hanging. The result is warm and welcoming, a charming space for relaxing and informal entertaining.

lighting

lighting

Today we don't give a second thought to flicking a switch and getting instant light, so we can only imagine the excitement surrounding the visit of the Prince and Princess of Wales in 1884 to a certain country mansion in Northumberland. They had come to Cragside to see why it was called 'the home of a modern magician'.

They were greeted by the sight of thousands of glass lamps and Chinese lanterns strung between the trees and brilliant rays of electric light from the newly invented filament bulbs, shining from every window. This was the home of Lord Armstrong, innovator and inventor, and the first house in the world to be lit by hydro-electricity. Those who saw it must have been, quite literally, dazzled.

Until the advances of gas and electricity, homes had depended on the naked flame for centuries – for rush lights (rushes, dipped in fat and dried) or oil lamps, for example. The fireplace was the main focus of domestic lighting but was also an opportunity for wealthy home owners to splash out on fabulous designs for chimneypieces, like the spectacular example depicting classical nymphs by Robert Adam at Croome.

Candles had been a principal form of lighting for poor and rich alike. Poor households used anything they could find as candlesticks – a hole in a loaf of bread would have sufficed on occasions. The wealthy could push the boat out with elaborate designs in gold, silver, pewter, carved wood and porcelain.

Cheap candles were made of tallow, or animal fat, which produced smoke and an unpleasant odour. Quality beeswax candles were virtually odourless and burned with a clear flame, but they were expensive; even the well-off were economical with candles and might only use one or two per evening when they were on their own.

When the wealthy entertained, however, it was a glittering affair. Hundreds of candles might be used in ballrooms and dining rooms and spectacular cut-glass chandeliers with multi-faceted droplets and beads would intensify the light and produce stunning effects. Gilt mirrors and picture frames would be placed strategically and even furnishing fabrics and clothes were sewn with silver and gold thread to catch the light.

Opposite: 18th century Rococo pier-glass and table at Ickworth.

Above: Page from a catalogue by Lea, Sons and Co. of Shrewsbury showing light fittings supplied to Cragside.

Below: Nymphs decorating the chimneypiece at Croome.

lighting types

There are three main types of lighting to think about when planning your room scheme, deciding how to light it and which fittings to choose:

- General or background lighting illuminates the overall space. This could be overhead lights or wall-mounted lights.
- Task lighting illuminates an activity such as reading or writing, so it could be a lamp on a desk, for example.
- Accent lighting draws attention to one or more objects and makes them a focal point. It could be a picture light over a painting or a spotlight on a vase display.

Right: The library at Mompesson House shows how a variety of light sources not only illuminates the room, but draws the eye to the architectural features and decoration. Walls painted white make the most of reflected light and are a cool contrast to the richness of the furnishings and carpet.

Below: This bathroom at The Homewood shows the use of borrowed light through glass brick walls.

lighting ideas

Bring in more light by choosing reflective surfaces such as chrome, glass and ceramic tiles.

Make a feature of paintings and prints on the wall by installing picture lights over them.

If you have a narrow bedroom without room for bedside lamps, add a shelf behind the headboard for a reading light and books.

Candles are perfect for creating a soft, romantic effect but be sure to place them somewhere safe, away from flammable objects and where there's no risk of them being knocked over.

reflected light

Practical and decorative, mirrors offer plenty of ways to make the most of the light. Use mirrors in any room that is small or dark, since reflected light will make it appear larger. Mirrors placed opposite windows are especially effective for reflecting light back into a room.

Here at Clandon Park (above) a mirror reflects the light but also the plaster bust on the pedestal, giving the corner some added interest. This creamy colour scheme is a perfect complement to the dark wood of the mirror frame.

At Felbrigg Hall (above) an enchantingly pretty but simple mirror frame against a soft lilac wall is embellished with Rococo-style plasterwork in the form of ribbons and fruit. A matching design can be seen reflected on the opposite wall.

Mirrored wardrobes provide obvious practical uses but also help to increase the feeling of space in a room. Here at Anglesey Abbey (above) the wardrobe is painted cream to enhance a light and airy mood.

A large gilt-framed mirror adds an elegant touch to the comfortable bedroom at Greenway (above) and reflects the plump cushions and accessories.

This gorgeous ceiling light (above) at Coleton Fishacre is unmistakably Art Deco, but it's a style that suits a variety of interiors. The gold tassels add a jazzy, opulent touch.

the light fantastic

Antique or vintage lamps and light fittings can bring wonderful period style to your home, but check that they have been professionally re-wired to modern safety standards. Alternatively, replicas of many original designs are also widely available.

The sinuous curves of Art Nouveau made it a popular choice for lamp designers. The cream frill and organic forms make this lamp at Arlington Court (right) a good partner for the wallpaper.

If you're after an industrial look for lighting, copper or brass lamps are a smart choice (above), and will add to the atmosphere by reflecting the light with a warm glow.

An Arts and Crafts lampshade at Standen is pleated and frilled with dark green silk (above), creating a romantic atmosphere. Arts-and-Crafts style lighting fits into many different room styles and there is a wide variety of designs to choose from.

Far left: Today, glass candle holders are available in similar styles to these lamp lights at Penrhyn Castle. Lined up along a mantelpiece or on a dining table, they bring a magical glow to an evening setting.

Left: The simplest objects can be enhanced by light. An enchanting effect is achieved by placing a jug of green bay leaves on the windowsill, where the soft glow gives them an ethereal quality.

a light touch

Above: A contemporary decorative glass hanging catches the light in front of the window, its pressed leaves and petals echoing the garden beyond.

Above: By day, there is optimum light from the full-height windows at The Homewood. A standard lamp beside the chair provides light for reading in the evening.

Above: Ernö Goldfinger designed a plain white bedroom scheme at 2 Willow Road, which includes an anglepoise lamp on each side of the bed. To help illuminate the en-suite bathroom, he created a light well in the ceiling.

romantic schemes

From candles to chandeliers, lighting can help you create an intimate mood in a room.

The vaulted dining room at Lindisfarne (above left) shows an irresistible setting for a meal, with the glow from candle bulbs on the far wall and a chandelier ready to light up the evening's festivities.

The powder room at The Homewood (above) is an atmospheric space, with glass blocks filtering soft rays of light, and the cylindrical glass hanging lights giving a sumptuous effect.

The lamps by the bed at Godolphin holiday cottage (above) cast pools of light on to the wall-hanging behind and the decorative frieze above. Cream lamp shades make a crisp contrast to the richly patterned rugs and dark wood furniture.

Patrick Gwynne's masterly use of light at The Homewood (above) makes the staircase full of contrast and interest. The big picture windows flood the space with light and the floor tiles and staircase reflect it further. Despite the Modernist architecture, a crystal chandelier gives a stylish nod to the ornamentation of the past with its Venetian blue-and-white glass leaf and flower embellishments.

natural light

Make the most of natural light by ensuring curtains can be drawn right back. Keep curtains simple – or dispense with them altogether – to make a feature of decorative or picture windows.

Glass-panelled doors have made the most of the natural light at Coleton Fishacre (right) and allow views of the garden from the dining room and the loggia beyond. The smooth blue marble-effect glass top table gleams as the light bounces across it.

Light floods into the room through the big sash windows at Hinton Ampner (above), making this niche the perfect spot for a writing desk. A well-placed lamp allowed the space to be used after dark.

With no curtains or blinds, this decorative arched window at Saltram (above) permits natural light to enhance the cool, serene décor of pale blue walls and white-painted chairs.

accessories

accessories

Accessories are the perfect finishing touch to a decorative scheme; they complement the room, adding extra colour, texture and interest. As with their fashion equivalents – handbags, scarves and jewellery – they help to bring the whole look together.

The interiors of historic houses of many periods show the owners' love of accessories. The wealthy could afford to embellish their rooms with cushions, tassels and tie backs and if you had expensive rugs there was no better way to show them off than to pose on them for your portrait. In many cases accessories were not only decorative but had practical purposes too, such as folding screens and fire screens.

Accessories reached their zenith in the Victorian home, where every chair, chaise-longue and sofa was heaped with piles of different cushions, throws and shawls. Tables were adorned with velvet-fringed cloths, framed photographs, cards, trinkets, souvenirs and smoking paraphernalia, while mantelpieces and dressing tables were festooned with lace edgings.

soft furnishings

Cushions, bolsters and throws offer cost-effective ways to finish off a scheme and are easily updated to reflect changing tastes and fashions.

Bring extra detail and interest to a corner of a room with a pile of soft, comfortable cushions. Here at Arlington Court (below) the muted colours and floral themes blend with each other and the trellis-effect wallpaper.

Pep up a decorative scheme by adding richly patterned cushions to plain upholstered furniture (above).

At Standen, the floral and botanical themes for the cushions on the steamer chairs echo their garden-like surroundings in the stunning conservatory (above).

folding screens

Folding screens date back to ancient China and have been a popular feature in historic homes for a variety of purposes. Not only did they help to keep draughts at bay before the arrival of central heating, and provide privacy, they also offered designers the chance to create highly elaborate and decorative pieces in lacquer, tooled leather or carved wood. Smaller dummy boards and screens would also be used in front of a fireplace in the summer months to create a decorative feature.

The Victorians enjoyed the pastime of making 'scrap screens', which originated from the Georgian print rooms of the 18th century. They would decorate their screens with a variety of pictures including animals, birds, cartoons and caricatures, cut out from magazines, newspapers and greetings cards.

Folding screens make a great accessory for any style of interior; they can be used to break up a large space, to conceal unsightly features such as pipework and cables or simply to add some portable pattern into a room. They are available in a wide choice of styles, including solid wood and partially glazed or lightweight frames covered in fabric or paper to match an existing scheme. They also come plain and unfinished, ready to paint and decorate.

Above: Folding screens bring colour and interest to a room, as shown in *A Quiet Half Hour* by Lionel Charles Henley at Hinton Ampner.

Above left: A patterned folding screen makes a pretty accessory in the nursery at Wightwick Manor. For children's rooms a screen can be practical, concealing toys and games when they're not in use, or they can serve as part of the fun of hide and seek. Why not encourage kids to help decorate a plain screen with their own designs?

Above: This bedroom at Scotney Castle includes an original Victorian scrap screen which has made a delightful addition to the colour scheme and adds an extra feminine touch.

Above: Contemporary meets traditional at Monk's House, where a folding screen printed with a graphic design adds striking contrast to the country-style kitchen. A screen can be a useful addition in a small room to hide items where there's no storage space.

vintage style

Today, vintage style is all the rage and it's easy to bring in a little retro chic to finish off your decorative scheme. Look for original pieces at antique shops, auctions, online dealers and second-hand fairs.

Nothing lends a vintage touch quite like a Bakelite telephone (above) seen here at Plas Newydd – but equally the artistry of their design makes them a stylish accessory in contemporary settings too.

Enjoy a little glamour from the great days of travel with vintage luggage (above). From large trunks to small overnight cases, they're great for all kinds of storage needs. Some still have their original address labels and stamps, which add to their charm.

In the past, many bedrooms had a dressing-table, adorned with brushes, combs and perfume bottles (above). Bring a little romance back with these decorative and practical accessories and add a lace table cover for extra glamour.

A sumptuous and relaxing retreat has been created at Kingston Lacy (above), where accessories provide some elegant finishing touches. A decorative white-painted mirror teams up with the Rococo-style bed and the floral-patterned sofa with plump cushions. A foldaway table has provided a place for the tea tray.

cover stars

The addition of cushions, patterned quilts, eiderdowns and throws to beds is a quick and easy way to accessorise a room.

The pale colours of the eiderdown and bed cover are soft and gentle against a pretty green upholstered headboard in this bedroom at Greenway (below).

Vibrant pink cushions and a purple throw on the bed add colour to a bedroom at Lower House holiday cottage (right). No further colour is needed for furnishings in this elegant neutral scheme, leaving the smart antique furniture to be the main attraction.

collections and displays

collections and displays

Nothing tells us more about the personalities and tastes of historic house owners than their collections. From fine art and antiquities to strange and unusual curiosities, displays and collections are an important part of the decorative spirit of the home.

Many wealthy young gentlemen, and some ladies, of the 18th century set off on the 'Grand Tour' to the Continent. This was an opportunity to immerse themselves in the cultural history of Europe, and to gather paintings, sculpture and other treasures that would later form the basis of some of the greatest private and national museum collections in the land. Some country-house owners built or remodelled large rooms

or entire wings in which to show off their magnificent displays. At Attingham Park, for example, architect John Nash was commissioned to create a superb picture gallery for his client.

Small and unusual objects and mementoes demanded a special kind of display in 'cabinets of curiosities'. These might include items that travellers had acquired from exotic places, or even old coins dug up from their own back gardens. At A La Ronde, the sixteen-sided Georgian home built by cousins Jane and Mary Parminter, the cabinet of curiosities includes a squirrel tail, ivory animals, shells and miniature books.

Today, few people have the inclination – or space – to collect on the scale of those in the past, but most of us have favourite objects, pictures and souvenirs that bring pleasure and we want to display and enjoy them. They enliven a room, allow us to indulge our creativity and stamp our personality on our homes.

Left: The 18th-century trend for collecting is depicted Wenzel Wehrlin's *A Collector in his Study*, at Wimpole Hall.

Top, right: A dark green-painted windowsill makes a striking backdrop for small decorative objects. The vase of bright red flowers adds extra impact.

Top, far right: Light filtering through a collection of coloured glass draws the eye and creates a stunning display at Sissinghurst Castle.

Right: A variety of glass bottles in different sizes and textures can achieve a simple but elegant effect on a small shelf.

Far right: Pretty patterned notebooks, a sprig of flowers and a framed photograph give the impression of a still life and echo the colours in the wallpaper and painted furniture.

kitchen displays

Open shelves in a kitchen offer the perfect opportunity to add a touch of style with displays of everyday objects.

The bright red kitchen wall at Scotney Castle (above) is matched by the pretty storage jars and crockery on the open shelves. Look out for plates and cups in different designs but in the same colour and create your own unique collection.

A traditional kitchen can be enhanced by displays of vintage metal moulds and copper pans (above). Copper pans can also be displayed from a hanging rack, so even if you are short of shelf space you can still create an attractive display.

A touch of humour is created on a kitchen shelf, where a picture of a bowl of lemons is displayed next to the real thing (above).

Practical and colourful, a set of retro cups and saucers makes a cheery display in a wicker basket (above).

displays in the home

In the summer months fireplaces are a great focus for a display of colourful pots or vases of dried or fresh flowers.

Bring contrast to a display by juxtaposing small and large or light and dark objects.

Displays aren't necessarily a finishing touch; a colourful painting or vase, for example, can be the starting point for a scheme and determine the colours for the decoration.

Think about the background for a display – a collection might look better on a wooden dresser or against a plain-coloured wall rather than large-patterned wallpaper.

One light-coloured object against a dark wall – or vice versa – can inject drama and impact into a scheme.

Create a still-life effect by grouping a variety of different objects together. A mix of old and new can provide a quirky touch.

Domed glass cloches, popular with the Victorians for protecting their plant specimens, make an interesting way to give focus and impact to a special item.

Objects in the same material look great together, such as an assortment of glass decanters or wooden carvings.

displays with style

Collections of objects add personality to a room. Arrange them by colour or theme for extra impact.

Lines of poetry by Tennyson have been painted on to a fire-surround at Wightwick Manor (above) and make a delightful accompaniment to the display of objects and figurines.

Green-and-white wallpaper and a border depicting shells and ships is a clever choice for a background to nautical pictures and ornaments as seen at Overbecks (above).

A selection of leather cases and hat boxes at Berrington Hall (above) is a practical as well as stylish period display.

A group of favourite pieces is given pride of place and lit by elegant lamps in the hallway at Antony (above). Notice how the symmetrical arrangement adds formality but the unusual combination of items makes the passer-by stop for a closer look.

favourite collections

Think about how your collections are going to be viewed and choose areas of the room where you can make them a focal point.

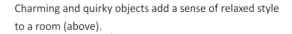

Charming and quirky objects add a sense of relaxed style to a room (above).

A corner-hung display shelf with pretty white and gold detailing makes a perfect backdrop to show off delicate pieces of porcelain (above).

Favourite small objects and trinkets look united when all displayed together (above).

The top of this bookshelf at Greenway has been decorated with an unusual collection of objects, echoed in a mirror of similar colour and texture (above).

setting up a display

Achieve an informal look by propping pictures against a wall or on a mantelpiece. For a stylish touch, display an empty carved or gilt frame, making the frame the art.

Make the most of a favourite object or collection with strategically placed lamps, spotlights or picture lights.

Show treasured or precious objects in glass-fronted display cabinets or glass-topped display tables.

Before hanging a group of pictures on the wall, lay them on the floor and move them around to help you decide on your final arrangement.

Mix the old and the new – antiques can look just as stunning in contemporary settings.

For any treasured or valuable object or collection, take expert advice on suitable care and conditions for its display.

picture displays

**From contemporary posters and black-and-white prints to
watercolours and oil paintings, pictures add personality to an interior.
They can also alter the mood of a room depending on the way they
are displayed, from cool and contemporary to rich and traditional.**

Photographer Edward Chambré Hardman hung photographs
to dry in his studio (below). Why not copy the idea and make
a display of photographs or postcards hung from clips for an
informal look?

A difference in scale can make a stylish display with a humorous
touch, where a large painting is hung above a miniature
(below), while at Wimpole Hall pictures with different themes
and in various sizes create a striking feature (right).

suppliers and further inspiration

This is a selection of suppliers offering products that can help you get the look for interiors seen in this book. For many other choices, check out high-street stores, online sites, antiques markets and charity shops.

Abdy Antiques
Vintage British telephones.
abdyantiques.co.uk
01709 578008

Andrew Martin
Innovative ranges of fabrics and wallpapers plus furniture, lighting and accessories.
andrewmartin.co.uk
020 7225 5100

And So To Bed
Beds inspired by historical designs, including French style, Victorian brass beds and four posters.
andsotobed.co.uk
0808 144 4343

Annie Sloan
Range of chalk paints plus waxes, varnishes and other materials.
anniesloan.com
01865 247296

Arc Prints
Reproduction prints with themes including classical, botanical and landscapes, and print-room effect fabrics, wallpaper and borders.
arcprints.com
020 7720 1628

Beaumont & Fletcher
Wall-lights and mirrors based on 18th and 19th century designs, and fabrics, wallpapers and hand-made furniture.
beaumontandfletcher.com
020 7352 5594

Bennison Fabrics
Fabrics based on original 18th and 19th century English and French textiles.
bennisonfabrics.com
020 7730 8076

Chelsea Textiles
Fabrics and cushions, including re-creations of antique embroidered textiles.
chelseatextiles.com
020 7584 0111

Cloud 9 Art Deco
Original Art Deco furniture and accessories.
cloud9artdeco.co.uk
01257 473 688

Colefax and Fowler
Fabrics and wallpapers which epitomise English style, including some of John Fowler's classic floral chintzes.
colefax.com
020 7244 7427

Crucial Trading
Floor coverings and rugs, including coir, sisal and seagrass.
crucial-trading.com
01562 743 747

Designers Guild
Ranges of fabrics and wallpapers, including vibrant florals, stripes and plains, plus furniture and home accessories.
designersguild.com
020 7351 5775

Farrow & Ball
Traditional paints and handcrafted wallpapers.
farrow-ball.com
01202 876141

Fired Earth
Wall and floor tiles, wallpapers and paint, including a National Trust-inspired range.
firedearth.com
0845 293 8798

Fritz Fryer
Antique chandeliers and lamps and bespoke, hand-made lighting collection.
fritzfryer.co.uk
01989 567416

GP & J Baker
Fabrics and wallpapers, including Far Eastern influences, damasks, embroideries and archive designs.
gpjbaker.com
01202 266700

Hamilton Weston
Wallpapers based on historic archives, including Georgian, Regency and Victorian designs.
hamiltonweston.com
020 8940 4850

Hines Tapestries
Tapestry wall-hangings, cushions and accessories based on medieval, Renaissance and Arts and Crafts designs.
hines-tapestries.com
01865 741144

Ian Mankin
Fabrics and wallpapers, including tickings, stripes, checks and plains.
ianmankin.co.uk
020 7722 0997

Jali
Custom-made furniture, including decorative shutters, folding screens and pelmets.
jali.co.uk
01227 833333

Jane Churchill
Traditional and contemporary ranges of fabrics and wallpapers including nautical, abstract and stripes.
janechurchill.com
020 7244 7427

Jim Lawrence
Hand-crafted light fittings, lamps, candelabra, curtain poles and other accessories.
jim-lawrence.co.uk
01473 826685

Lassco
Architectural antiques, salvage and curiosities, including reclaimed flooring, doors and chimneypieces.
lassco.co.uk
020 7394 2100

Lewis & Wood
Wallpapers including print-room designs, nautical themes, marbled effects and toile de Jouy.
lewisandwood.co.uk
01453 878517

Lincrusta
Wall coverings, friezes, dado panels, borders, and ideas for achieving decorative effects.
www.lincrusta.com
01254 222803

Little Greene
Traditional paints and wallpapers including designs inspired by originals from the 18th century to the 1970s.
littlegreene.com
0845 880 5855

Morris & Co
Fabrics and wallpapers in William Morris and 'Morris and Co' designs alongside new interpretations.
william-morris.co.uk
0844 543 9500

National Trust Prints

Framed or canvas prints from images in the National Trust's picture library including portraits, landscapes, gardens, architecture and interiors.

ntprints.com

Original Style

Floor and wall tiles, in glass, mosaics and natural stone including Victorian floor tiles based on original patterns.

originalstyle.com
01392 473000

Osborne & Little

Wallpapers and fabrics including silks, velvets and weaves.

osborneandlittle.com
020 7352 1456

Paint and Paper Library

Paints inspired by historical, traditional and contemporary interiors.

paintlibrary.co.uk
020 7590 9860

Painted Wall Panelling

Made-to-measure, ready-to-paint wall panelling, including Georgian, Victorian and Arts and Crafts designs.

paintedwallpanelling.com
0121 328 1643

Papers and Paints

Wide range of paints and accessories; consultancy on the painted decoration of historical buildings.

papers-paints.co.uk
020 7352 8626

Paris Ceramics

Tiled flooring including limestone flags, terracotta tiles and decorative ceramics.

parisceramics.com
020 7371 7778

Roger Oates

Contemporary pure-wool flat-weave runners and rugs, and fabrics.

rogeroates.com
01531 632718

Romo

Contemporary and classic design collections including vibrant floral fabrics and velvet flock and metallic finish wallpapers.

romo.com
01623 756699

Rugs of the World

Tribal rugs and kilims, Aubusson rugs and a wide range of traditional and contemporary designs.

rugsoftheworld.net
01904 676660

Sanderson

Coordinating wallpapers and fabrics, classic florals and archive-inspired designs, 1950s and bold contemporary collections.

sanderson-uk.com
0844 543 9500

Scumble Goosie

Ready-to-paint and bespoke furniture plus clocks, mirrors and accessories.

scumblegoosie.co.uk
01453 731305

Simon Horn

Beds inspired by historic styles including Rococo, Empire, Regency and American Colonial.

simonhorn.com
020 7731 1279

Stevensons of Norwich

Decorative plasterwork mouldings including the National Trust range of cornices.

stevensonsofnorwich.com
01603 400824

The Conran Shop

Furniture and accessories including 20th century design classics by Charles & Ray Eames, Mies van der Rohe and Arne Jacobsen.

conranshop.co.uk
0844 848 4000

The Dormy House

Bespoke and ready-to-finish furniture and accessories including folding screens and dressing tables.

thedormyhouse.com

01264 365808

The Stencil Library

Decorative stencils including Medieval, Gothic, Neo-classical, Arts and Crafts and Art Deco designs, plus glazes, varnishes and accessories.

stencil-library.co.uk

01661 844844

Titley and Marr

Fabric collections including range of toile de Jouy designs.

titleyandmarr.co.uk

02392 599585

Vaughan

Lighting including wall and floor lamps and chandeliers, plus fabrics and accessories.

vaughandesigns.com

020 7349 4600

Victorian Ceramics

Wall and fireplace tiles including authentic reproductions of designs by William Morris, William de Morgan and Philip Webb.

victorianceramics.com

01746 710534

Watts

Wallpapers and fabrics from original patterns including designs by Pugin.

watts1874.co.uk

020 7376 4486

Zoffany

Contemporary and classic designs for wallpaper and fabrics including plains, stripes, silks and weaves.

zoffany.com

0844 543 4600

national trust holiday cottages

Some of the inspiring images in this book come from the National Trust's holiday houses, apartments and cottages. For further information:

nationaltrustcottages.co.uk

0844 800 20 70

organisations and groups

Lapada – The Association of Art and Antique Dealers

lapada.org

SPAB (The Society for the Protection of Ancient Buildings)

spab.org.uk

020 7377 1644

English Heritage

english-heritage.org.uk

0870 333 1181

The Traditional Paint Forum

traditionalpaintforum.org.uk

The Victorian Society

victoriansociety.org.uk

020 8994 1019

The Georgian Group

georgiangroup.org.uk

087 1750 2936

The Twentieth Century Society

c20society.org.uk

020 7250 3857

index

acknowledgements

I would especially like to thank John Stachiewicz, Grant Berry and Chris Lacey at the National Trust and Cathy Gosling, Kristy Richardson and Lucy Smith at Anova for their encouragement, help and advice throughout the production of this book. I am grateful to a number of staff at National Trust central and regional offices and at properties who offered help and expertise, with special thanks to Nicola Jackson at National Trust Holiday Cottages, and to Christine Sitwell, Oliver Garnett, James Grasby, Katy Lithgow and Emile de Bruijn. I also want to thank family and friends for their help, especially Winifred Dalby, Colm O'Kelly, Cressida O'Kelly, Jonathan Downs and Siân Evans. And above all, my sincere thanks for all her support and encouragement to my friend Jacq Barber.

picture credits

1